MICHAEL

Don't
What To Do

Retold by Philip King

HEINEMANN

ELEMENTARY LEVEL

Series Editor: John Milne

The Heinemann Guided Readers provide a choice of enjoyable reading material for learners of English. The series is published at five levels – Starter, Beginner, Elementary, Intermediate and Upper. At **Elementary Level**, the control of content and language has the following main features:

Information Control
Stories have straightforward plots and a restricted number of main characters. Information which is vital to the understanding of the story is clearly presented and repeated when necessary. Difficult allusion and metaphor are avoided and cultural backgrounds are made explicit.

Structure Control
Students will meet those grammatical features which they have already been taught in their elementary course of studies. Other grammatical features occasionally occur with which the students may not be so familiar, but their use is made clear through context and reinforcement. This ensures that the reading as well as being enjoyable provides a continual learning situation for the students. Sentences are kept short – a maximum of two clauses in nearly all cases – and within sentences there is a balanced use of simple adverbial and adjectival phrases. Great care is taken with pronoun reference.

Vocabulary Control
At **Elementary Level** there is a limited use of a carefully controlled vocabulary of approximately 1,100 basic words. At the same time, students are given some opportunity to meet new or unfamiliar words in contexts where their meaning is obvious. The meaning of words introduced in this way is reinforced by repetition. Help is also given to the students in the form of vivid illustrations which are closely related to the text.

Contents

1 On My Own 4

2 A Job With Masters 8

3 Shirley 13

4 The Swimming Pool 16

5 My Bag is Searched 19

6 Something Very Valuable 21

7 Don't Tell Me What To Do 26

8 An Argument 30

9 A Lucky Escape 34

10 Learning to Use the Scuba Suit 38

11 A Man Called Lewis 42

12 The Job Begins 45

13 Inside *The Kular* 48

14 Questions Are Answered 54

Points for Understanding 59

List of titles at Elementary Level 63

1

On My Own

One morning I left home early. I did not say goodbye to my parents.

My father wanted me to work in an office. But I loved horses and I wanted to ride horses. I wanted to be a jockey, but my father didn't understand. So I left home. I was on my own.

I took a bus from the centre of town and then I walked. Soon I reached the motorway. I wanted to get to London, but I didn't have a car. Every time a car came, I put out my hand. But the cars didn't stop. Half an hour passed. And then my luck changed.

A big red Jaguar came up behind me. I saw the driver look at me. Then the car slowed down and stopped.

For a moment I was worried. Perhaps the driver was lost and wanted to ask me the way. But then he opened the door.

'Get in,' said the driver cheerfully. 'I can give you a lift. We're both going the same way.'

I got in and sat in the seat beside the driver. There was a girl sitting in the back. She had blonde hair and she didn't seem to be very tall. I thought that the girl looked older than me.

The driver started the car again and drove off quickly. I felt pleased for a moment. I had never been in a Jaguar before. It was a big, fast and comfortable car.

Then the driver turned and looked at me.

'Where are you going?' he asked.

'London,' I replied.

'Get in,' said the driver cheerfully. 'I can give you a lift.'

'Do you live there, or are you going to work there?' he asked.

'Well, yes,' I said.

'What do you mean, "yes"?' he asked me.

'I don't live in London. I'm going to work in London.'

'What is your job?' he asked.

He was asking a lot of questions and I didn't want to answer them. I was afraid of his questions because I didn't want to talk about myself. So I didn't answer him. I said nothing.

'I'm sorry,' he said with a smile. 'Am I asking you too many questions?'

I was surprised. How did he know what I was thinking? I wasn't able to think of a good answer, and I said simply, 'No, no, that's all right. I don't mind telling you things.'

'Well, good,' the driver said. 'It's much better to talk when you're travelling together. It's better than sitting in silence for hours. I like young people.'

I didn't say anything. I remembered the girl in the back. Why didn't she speak? Was she his daughter? I didn't know. Perhaps she was his wife. But why was she sitting in the back? A wife doesn't sit in the back when her husband is driving.

I still had my bag in my arms.

'Why don't you put your bag in the back?' asked the driver. 'You'll be more comfortable then.'

I turned round and put the bag in the back. I looked at the girl. She was very pretty. She smiled. I saw that she wasn't very tall.

'Her name's Shirley,' said the driver. 'And I'm Vincent

Masters. What's your name?'

'Tom,' I said, 'Tom Doggett.'

'Hello, Tom,' said the girl, Shirley. She spoke in a very friendly way. I was sure that she liked me.

'Where's your home?' Masters asked me.

'Oh, near Liverpool,' I replied. This wasn't exactly true. I didn't live near Liverpool. I lived in Liverpool. But I didn't want him to learn anything about me.

'Oh, yes,' he said. 'I know Liverpool very well. I have a lot of friends there. Do you live with your parents?'

I was waiting for this question. And I had thought of an answer.

'I haven't got any parents,' I said quickly.

'Oh, I'm sorry,' said Masters. 'Have your parents been dead long?'

'Two years. They were killed in a car crash,' I replied. 'My father was driving. The other car came straight at him. He was killed immediately.'

'That's terrible,' Masters said. 'There are far too many accidents these days.'

Masters believed my story. It wasn't true, of course. My parents were still alive, but I wanted to forget them. I had left home. I was on my own now.

'Do you live on your own, or with relatives?' Masters asked.

'On my own,' I said. 'I have my own flat.'

'That's good,' Masters said. 'Not many boys like you have their own flat. How old are you, Tom?'

'Seventeen,' I said, 'nearly eighteen.'

I was pleased because Masters believed everything I told him. I told him the truth and he believed me. I told him a lie and he still believed me.

The car drove on, and he didn't ask me any more questions. I hoped that Masters was going to London. But I still didn't know. He hadn't told me.

Suddenly he slowed down. The car turned off the motorway. And we were still a long way from London.

2

A Job With Masters

'Here's a café,' Masters said. 'I feel hungry. Shall we have something to eat and drink?'

'Fine,' Shirley said.

I didn't want to stop. I wanted to get to London quickly. But I didn't say anything. Masters was already getting out of the car. So I got out too.

Shirley got out and smiled at me. I saw that she wasn't very tall. In fact, we were the same height. I was sure that she liked me.

We all went into the café. Shirley went and sat at a table by the window. I sat opposite her because I wanted to look at her.

Then Masters came. He was carrying three cups of tea and some sandwiches on a tray. He sat down next to me. I was surprised. Why didn't he sit next to Shirley? So he isn't very friendly with her, I thought.

We ate our sandwiches quietly for a few minutes. Then Masters spoke to me.

'Have you a good job in London, Tom?'

*He was carrying three cups of tea and some sandwiches
on a tray.*

I didn't know what to say. I didn't have a job in London.

'Oh, yes, I'm sure that it will be,' I said.

'What exactly will your job be?' he asked.

I didn't want to say any more; but it was difficult to say nothing. Masters was being very friendly. Well, I thought, I can say anything. It doesn't matter. When we get to London, I'll never see him again.

'I'm going to be a jockey,' I told him.

'Yes,' said Masters. He smiled. 'You're the right size to be a jockey, aren't you. It must be a very interesting job for a young man. But it's hard work, very hard work. And you've got to be strong.'

'I am strong,' I said. 'When I was at school, I was stronger than many of the bigger boys.'

'Yes, I'm not surprised,' replied Masters. 'You look strong to me. Small people like you are often very strong.'

I was pleased when Masters said this. Most people looked at me and laughed because I was so short. But Masters knew that I was strong.

'Who are you going to ride for?' Masters asked.

I didn't understand his question.

So he explained to me. A jockey works for a man who owns racehorses. The jockey rides his horses.

'Well, I haven't decided yet,' I said.

'Do you know any racehorse owners?' Masters asked.

'No,' I said, 'I don't.'

'But there are so many young men like you, Tom,' said Masters. 'They all want to be jockeys. You won't find a job easily. You must know a racehorse owner.'

Masters was right.

'And you'll need money in London,' he said. 'You won't get a job immediately. Have you got much money?'

'A little,' I said.

Masters was right again: I needed money. But where was I going to get money?

'It takes a very long time to become a real jockey,' said Masters. 'You'll work for a long time before you earn much money. I know. I used to own racehorses myself. I had one or two jockeys. But they didn't get much money.'

Now I was very interested in Masters. So he had owned racehorses. Perhaps he'll be able to help me, I thought.

'What about your weight?' Masters asked me. 'How much do you weigh?'

'Forty-three kilos,' I said.

'Forty-three kilos,' said Masters. 'You're a little too heavy for a jockey. You'll have to lose some weight, you know.'

It's not going to be easy to become a jockey, I thought.

'Do you swim?' Masters asked suddenly.

'Yes, I like swimming,' I said.

'Good,' he said. 'Swimming is good for you. It's good exercise and it makes you strong. Shirley likes swimming too.'

Shirley looked at me and smiled. I felt happy again. I liked Shirley and I liked Masters. They were kind to me and they were interested in me.

'Look, Tom,' Masters said, 'I can help you. You need money now, don't you? And I have a job for you, if you want it. But not as a jockey. Work for me for a fortnight and I'll give you one thousand pounds.'

'What's the job?' I asked.

'I can't explain to you now,' Masters said. 'It's difficult to explain. But come home with me now, and I can show you. You can live in my house. When you have one thousand pounds, you can live in London and look for work as a jockey.'

I thought about it. I needed the money.

'Yes,' I said, 'I'll do the job.'

'Good,' Masters said.

'Good,' Shirley said too. She smiled at me. 'I'll help you with this job. I also work for him, you know.'

'Well,' Masters said, 'can you start work today?'

'Yes,' I said.

'Let's go to my house now,' Masters said. 'Then we can talk about the job.'

'I'm glad that you're taking the job,' Shirley said, holding my hand. 'You'll do a very good job.'

Nobody had ever spoken such kind words to me.

We left the café and went back to the car. Immediately Masters started off for his home.

3

Shirley

The car turned off the road and along a narrow path. A minute later we stopped outside a big house. I had never seen such a beautiful house before. Masters is a very rich man, I thought to myself.

Shirley pointed towards some trees.

'There's a path there. It leads to the swimming pool,' she said. 'I'll show you later and we'll have a swim.'

There was a small field with some horses in it near one corner of the house. Perhaps Masters wanted me to work with the horses. I was able to see the sea about two kilometres away in the distance.

We went into the house and into a large room. The room was full of expensive-looking furniture. There were shelves full of books all round the walls. But where was Masters' wife? There didn't seem to be any other people in the house. It seemed to be empty. Perhaps Masters didn't have a wife.

'Make yourself at home, Tom,' Masters said in a friendly voice. 'What do you want to drink?'

'Some whisky, please,' I replied. I had never drunk whisky before, but I wanted to try some.

'Fine,' Masters said. 'Have a drink and then Shirley will show you your room. It's a nice room. You'll like it. We'll have a meal later. Shirley is a very good cook.'

I was surprised. What was Shirley's real job? Perhaps she was Masters' cook. I didn't know.

'We're going to work very well together,' said Masters.

'Yes,' I said. 'Tell me about the job. What do you want me to do?'

I had never seen such a beautiful house before.

'Later, Tom, I'll tell you later,' said Masters. 'Have a rest now. I'll tell you all about the job tomorrow. There's no hurry.'

But I wanted to find out more. And so I asked another question.

'Is it a dangerous job?'

'Why?' Masters asked me. 'Are you frightened?'

'No, of course not,' I replied. 'I don't want an easy job. I want an interesting job.'

'Good,' said Masters. 'I like that. No, it's not a dangerous job, but there are a few risks.'

I was not worried by a few risks. One thousand pounds was a lot of money.

Masters stood up. 'Well, now you can see your room,' he said. And at that moment Shirley came in.

'Show Tom his room, will you, Shirley?' Masters asked.

I followed Shirley up the stairs and along a corridor. My room had a bed and three chairs. There were also two lamps and some shelves with books. It was much better than my room at home.

'OK?' asked Shirley.

'Great,' I said. 'It's great.'

'That's my room,' Shirley said, and pointed to the next door.

I was pleased that her room was so near. I liked her very much.

'Do you want to go for a swim now?' she asked me. 'There's plenty of time before we eat.'

'Yes,' I said.

'I'll meet you at the pool in five minutes,' she said. 'Go down the path that I showed you.'

She went out and closed the door immediately. Then I

remembered something. I didn't have any swimming trunks. I wanted to find Shirley and ask her. I knocked on her door, but there was no answer. So I went to the pool and looked for her there.

4

The Swimming Pool

The swimming pool was very big and deep. There was a small hut beside it. I got to the pool and the door of the hut opened. Shirley came out. She was wearing a black swimming-costume and looked beautiful.

She saw me looking at her.

'Do you like it?' she asked.

I didn't know what to say. 'Yes, it's great,' I replied.

'Hurry up and get changed,' she said.

'But I haven't got any trunks,' I said.

'There are some trunks in the hut. Go and put them on.'

I went into the hut and changed. The trunks fitted me well. I dived into the water. Shirley swam to me and touched my arm.

'Let's have a race,' she said.

We raced to the other end of the pool and I won. I liked swimming and so I was enjoying myself now.

After a few minutes Shirley showed me a big ring.

'Let's have a game with this ring,' she said. 'I'll dive under the water with it. Then you try and swim through it. OK?'

She dived into the water and I swam down to her. The

ring was very close to the wall of the pool. There was not much room and I wasn't able to swim through it easily. I tried, but I was not able to get through. We both swam up to the surface.

'You'll have to do better next time,' Shirley said. Her voice was unfriendly. I was surprised. But I really was a good swimmer. I wanted her to see that.

We dived again. I was very careful this time. I swam through the ring once. Then I swam through the ring again. I was able to do it quite easily this time.

We got out of the pool.

'That was much better,' Shirley said with a big smile.

I wanted to hold her hand. But I was frightened. Perhaps she didn't want me to touch her. So I did nothing.

'Now something else,' she said after a few minutes.

'There's a large stone down at the bottom of the pool. Can you get it up and put it on the path?'

I didn't believe her. I hadn't seen any stone in the pool.

'Go on,' she ordered. Her voice was unfriendly again. 'Bring it up. Aren't you strong enough?'

I dived into the water again.

At last I saw the stone. I picked it up and swam to the surface. I tried to get the stone out, but it slipped and sank to the bottom.

'That's no good,' Shirley shouted angrily. 'Do it again! Do it properly!'

I was angry. Why was she giving me orders like this? I was working for Masters, not for Shirley.

But I was alone and I needed a friend. I didn't have any other friends now. Shirley liked me. I was sure of that. I dived again. This time I brought the stone up and got it onto the path.

'I didn't like that game,' I said. 'It wasn't easy.'

'It was hard,' Shirley said, 'but Masters is paying you for hard work.'

I was surprised. But before I said anything, she kissed me. So she really did like me! I kissed her and I forgot my anger. Then she suddenly drew back her head.

'Not now,' she said. 'I must go and get dinner ready. Masters is probably waiting for us.'

'Do you work for him all the time?' I asked her.

'Yes,' she replied.

'What do you do?' I asked. 'I mean, what is your real job?'

'I make myself useful,' she said.

'How does Masters make all his money?' I asked.

'You'll have to ask him yourself,' she said. 'He may tell you and he may not. You'd better get changed now, Tom. I'll see you in the house.'

And she walked away.

5

My Bag is Searched

I went and changed my clothes and then I walked back to the house. I was thinking all the time. Masters was paying me for hard work. But what work? Why did he want me?

I went up to my room. I met Masters on the way.

'Hello,' he said with a smile. 'Did you have a good swim?'

'Yes, thanks,' I said.

'Were you able to swim through the ring?' he asked.

So it was Masters' idea. He had arranged it all.

'Yes, I swam through the ring,' I said.

'Good,' said Masters. 'You did very well. I saw you from the window.'

He had seen me in the pool. Perhaps he had seen me kiss Shirley. I felt angry.

'Were you spying on us?' I asked.

'Of course not,' Masters replied. 'I saw you by chance. You can see the pool from my window upstairs.'

I still felt angry because I didn't really believe him. But I said nothing.

'Well, come and have some food,' he said. 'You must be hungry.'

We went into the dining-room and Shirley brought the food in. Then she went out again.

'Isn't she going to eat with us?' I asked Masters.

'Oh, she's busy,' said Masters. 'You'll see her again later.'

After we finished the meal, I asked Masters again about the job.

'We can talk about that tomorrow,' he said.

I still didn't know anything about Masters.

'What do you do?' I asked. 'What business are you in?' Masters looked at me for a moment.

'Salvage,' he said.

I didn't know what he meant. But I was to find out soon. Masters stood up.

'I have a lot of work to do now,' he said. 'Excuse me, but I must go. If you want, you can watch television. But go to bed soon and get plenty of sleep. You start work tomorrow morning.'

I watched televison for a short time. But Shirley didn't appear again and I felt tired. I decided to go to bed.

When I got to my room, I looked for my bag. I had left it on the bed, but now it was on a chair. I looked in the bag. Everything had been moved, but nothing was missing. Someone had been in my room and had gone through my things.

I sat down on the bed and thought to myself. It was Shirley, of course. I was sure of that. She hadn't eaten with us. She had been in my room when Masters and I were eating. She was spying on me. And Masters was spying on me too. But why? What did they want to find out?

I was very tired and I couldn't think clearly. I decided to speak to Shirley in the morning. The most important question was: What is the job that Masters wants me to do?

I'll know that in the morning, I thought, and then I fell asleep.

6

Something Very Valuable

'There it is,' Masters said to me. 'The ship is down there under the water.'

We had left Masters' house about two hours ago. We had driven down to the mouth of the river by car. Now we were sitting in a boat about two kilometres out at sea. Masters was pointing down at the water.

'The ship is called *The Kular*,' Masters was saying. 'It sank last month. When it sank, it turned on its side.

'*The Kular* was carrying something for me, something very valuable. It was a bag with diamonds in it. They're worth a lot of money, and they're important to me, too. I need them in my business. I've waited a long time for them.

'I've been down into the ship, Tom. I know where the diamonds are. But I couldn't get to them. It's very difficult because the ship is lying on its side. Only a small, strong man can get to them. I'm too big. That's why I need you, Tom. You're small enough to reach the diamonds.'

I didn't know what to say. I felt a bit afraid.

'You're not frightened, Tom, are you?' Masters asked.

'No, of course I'm not,' I said quickly.

'Good,' said Masters. 'There's no need to be afraid. I'll come down there with you. You'll be safe.'

So this was the job! Salvage. Masters wanted me to get the diamonds out of the sunken ship. I didn't know what to say. It did not seem an easy job to me.

'I've never stayed under the water for long,' I said. 'How can I dive down and get the diamonds?'

'You're a good swimmer,' Masters said. 'Come home with me and you can practise for a few days. You must have a scuba suit.'

'What's that?' I asked.

'A scuba suit is a special rubber suit for divers. It keeps you dry and warm under the water. You wear a mask on your face. And you carry the air on your back in a cylinder. Then you can stay under the water for twenty minutes.'

'But I'm not a diver. I've never used a scuba suit,' I said.

'That doesn't matter,' Masters said. 'I can train you. Shirley can help you. She has used a scuba suit.'

I was pleased to hear this. So I'll see her and work with her again, I thought.

'Let's go back now,' Masters said. 'There's nothing more to see for the moment.'

On the way back, I thought about the job. Masters had said that it was very simple. But it seemed a bit dangerous to me. Masters is going to give me one thousand pounds for the job, I thought to myself. Why don't I ask him for more money? I'll ask him for fifteen hundred pounds.

I decided to ask Masters for fifteen hundred pounds. I was on my own now. I had no family with me and no friends. I had to think of myself.

22

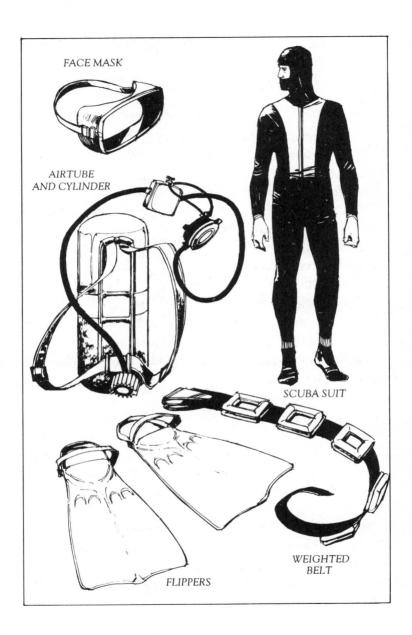

FACE MASK

AIRTUBE
AND CYLINDER

SCUBA SUIT

FLIPPERS

WEIGHTED
BELT

When we reached the mouth of the river, we tied up the boat and got out.

'Well, Tom, do you think you can do it?' Masters asked.

'Yes, I'm sure I can, Mr Masters,' I said, 'but . . .'

'Yes, what is it?' Masters asked.

'Well, I think the job is worth more than one thousand pounds,' I said.

Masters laughed. He seemed amused.

'Good,' he said. 'You'll make a good businessman. Tell me. How much do you think the job is worth?'

'I think fifteen hundred pounds,' I said. I was nervous. I hoped Masters did not see this.

Masters thought for a moment.

'That's a lot of money,' Masters said slowly. 'But you want to get the best for yourself. Good. All right, I agree. Get the diamonds and I'll give you fifteen hundred pounds.'

I felt much better now. Fifteen hundred pounds! That was a lot of money.

'When are we going to do the job?' I asked.

'On Sunday, I hope,' Masters said. 'It'll have to be early in the morning. Then there won't be so many people around. There won't be so many boats on the river. I don't want people to see us. No one must find out about the diamonds. That's why we came so early this morning.'

Was Masters telling the truth about everything? And why did he want everything to be secret? Perhaps it was because of the diamonds. I didn't know.

'Let's go now,' Masters said. 'I have to see a man called Clark. We can have a cup of coffee there.'

'Who's Clark?' I asked.

'He's going to help us on Sunday,' Masters replied. 'He lives near here so he can easily come and help us.'

'Won't Shirley be with us on Sunday?' I asked.

'Oh, yes, she'll be with us,' Masters said. 'You like her, Tom, don't you? Yes, of course you do. She likes you as well. You can take her out tonight. I'll give you the money. You can take her to a restaurant for a meal.'

'Thanks very much,' I said. I was pleased that she liked me.

We got to Clark's house and had coffee. Clark and Masters talked for a long time about Sunday and about the job. When we were in the car again, Masters spoke to me.

'I want you to do one thing, Tom.'

'What's that?' I asked.

'You must make a telephone call today, Tom.'

'Who to?' I asked.

'Oh, Shirley will explain,' Masters said. 'But it's very important. You must promise to make the telephone call.'

'All right,' I replied. 'But I don't understand.'

'You will understand, Tom,' Masters said. 'But don't think about it now. Shirley will explain later. You and I must do some work first.

'We're going to look at some plans of the ship this afternoon. You must study the plans carefully. Then you'll know where the diamonds are hidden. This is very important. When you're in the water, you'll have to find the diamonds quickly. And it'll be dark down in the water.'

I heard Masters, but I wasn't listening to him. I was thinking about the phone call. What was this phone call? And why did I have to make it?

7

Don't Tell Me What To Do

I worked with Masters all afternoon. We studied the plans of the ship. Masters showed me where the diamonds were. He explained how I could find them.

'Remember the plans very carefully,' he said. 'When you're on the ship, you must remember. You mustn't make a mistake.'

So I worked hard and studied the plans carefully. When we had finished, Masters spoke to me about the evening.

'You're taking Shirley out this evening, aren't you?' he said. 'You'll need some money. Here's £30. You'll need a car too. You can take my car. Not the Jaguar. I have a second car, a Mini. You can take that. You can drive, can't you?'

'Yes,' I said.

It was true. I could drive. But when you drive a car, you need a driving-licence. And I didn't have a driving-licence.

———

Shirley came downstairs. She was wearing an orange-coloured dress and she looked very beautiful. I couldn't believe I was going out with such a beautiful girl.

'Where shall we go?' I asked when we were in the car.

'Let's go to a pub and have a drink,' Shirley said.

When we had driven along the road for about two kilometres, Shirley pointed to a telephone box.

'Stop here,' she said.

'Why?' I asked.

'You have to make an important telephone call,' she said. 'Remember?'

'What phone call?'

'You must phone your father,' said Shirley.

'But I told you, my father's dead,' I said.

'No, Tom, that's not true. He's not dead.'

'You're mad,' I said. 'I told you he died in a car crash.'

'Stop it, Tom,' Shirley said. 'Your father's called Wilfred Doggett and he lives in Liverpool.'

'How do you know?' I asked. 'Were you spying on me?'

'No, Tom,' she said. 'But last night you talked in your sleep. You talked about your father. Masters heard you. He heard a lot of noise, and so he listened. You were shouting about your father. You said you hated your father. You said you didn't want to stay at home with him.'

So Masters knew the truth about me. But I didn't mind. I wasn't going back home. I wasn't going to see my father again.

'But why must I ring my father?' I said. 'I hate him. I don't want to ring him.'

'No, Tom, you must ring him,' Shirley said. 'Your father knows that you are missing now. Perhaps he'll call the police and the police will search for you. So you must ring your father. Tell him that you have a good job and you are well. Then your father won't worry about you.'

Shirley was right.

'You understand, don't you?' she said. And she gave me a kiss. 'Now make the phone call, please, Tom.'

'Oh, no, not now, Shirley,' I said.

'Tom, please make the phone call now. Then we can forget all about your father and we can enjoy the evening. It's very easy. Just tell your father that you have a good job. Tell him that you'll write to him soon.'

'All right,' I said. 'Don't tell me what to do. I know what

I'm going to say.'

'Good,' she said. 'Here's some money for the phone call.'

'I've got money,' I said.

I left Shirley in the car and went over to the telephone. I had enough money to speak for two minutes. I didn't want to talk for long to my father. I telephoned.

'Mr Doggett speaking,' said my father's voice.

'This is Tom,' I said. 'Look, I've got a good job . . .'

'Tom, my boy, where are you?' my father asked. 'Your mother and I are so worried.'

'I'm in Manchester,' I said. This was not true, of course. 'Listen, I have a good job here. Don't worry about me. I'll write to you next week.'

'But what's your address? Give me your address,' my father said.

'Look, I have to go,' I said. 'I'm in a phone box and I haven't got any more money for the phone.'

'Wait, Tom, wait,' my father said. 'Don't put the phone down. Give me your phone number and I'll . . .'

'Sorry,' I said. 'No time. I'll write to you next week. Goodbye.'

I put the phone down and went back to Shirley. I was glad I had finished the call.

'Well done,' she said. 'Now let's go to the pub.'

8

An Argument

We drove to the next village and stopped at the pub. It was an old building. I knew that old pubs like this one were expensive. I parked the car in a car-park full of big, expensive cars. I didn't like this pub much.

We went in. The pub was full and there were no seats.

'I don't mind. I'll stand up,' said Shirley.

I went to the bar and ordered some drinks.

'Excuse me, sir, but are you over eighteen?' asked the man behind the bar. 'You must be over eighteen, or I can't give you any drinks. That's the law, you know.'

'Of course I'm over eighteen,' I shouted angrily.

Everyone looked at me. The man gave me the drinks and I took them back to Shirley.

'You were a long time,' she said.

I didn't answer. I still felt angry with the man.

There was silence. Then Shirley spoke to me.

'What did your father say on the phone?' she asked.

I didn't reply to her question. I didn't want to talk about my father. I drank some beer but it didn't taste very nice.

Suddenly Shirley smiled. I looked around. A young man was coming towards us. I felt annoyed. Who was he? Why was Shirley smiling at him?

'Hi, Christopher,' she said.

'You're looking lovely tonight,' he said and kissed her.

Shirley turned to me.

'Christopher, this is Tom,' she said. 'Tom, meet Christopher.'

I parked the car in a car-park full of big, expensive cars.
I didn't like this pub much.

'Sorry,' said Christopher, 'I didn't realise you had a friend with you, Shirley.' And he smiled.

I didn't like the way he said the word 'friend'. I didn't like his smile. Now I was feeling really angry.

'I'll go and get myself a drink,' said Christopher.

He turned around. As he turned, he knocked over my glass. Some of the beer spilt over my trousers and shoes.

Without thinking, I tried to hit Christopher. I missed, and Christopher tried to hit me. A woman shouted.

'Tom, stop it,' Shirley shouted.

I was still holding my glass. I wanted to push it into Christopher's face.

The man came from behind the bar.

'This isn't the place for a fight,' he said angrily. 'Finish your drink quietly and get out.'

I was very angry now, and my face was red. I wanted to hit the barman, but Shirley stopped me.

'Stop it, Tom,' she said. 'That's enough. Come on, let's go.'

'Look, Shirley, it wasn't my fault,' I said. 'I'm sorry.'

But she was already walking towards the door and I followed her.

'You were stupid, stupid,' said Shirley when we were outside. 'You were like a stupid child in there.'

Shirley got into the car and closed the door. I got in too.

'Come on, let's go,' she said.

We drove away quickly, and started to go very fast along the road.

'Who's Christopher?' I asked.

'He's a friend – someone I know,' Shirley said. 'Why were you so angry with him?'

'Why did he kiss you?' I asked.

'It was nothing, nothing at all,' she said. 'He's just a friend.'

'Really?' I said. 'I didn't think so.'

'You don't understand,' Shirley said. 'You don't have the same sort of friends as me.'

That was true.

We stopped talking. I was enjoying driving the car now and it was going fast. I looked across at Shirley.

When I looked ahead again, there was a bend in the road in front. I hadn't seen it because I was looking at Shirley. I put my foot down hard on the brake.

The car went across to the other side of the road. For a moment, I thought that it was going off the road. I needed all my strength to control the car.

'Slow down, you fool!' Shirley shouted.

I was trying to slow down. I managed to keep the car on the road, and we went round the corner.

'That's better,' I said. 'We're all right now.'

But we weren't all right. I heard a noise behind us. Shirley turned round.

'It's a police-car, Tom,' she said. 'It's coming up behind us. They want us to stop.'

And I didn't have a driving-licence!

9

A Lucky Escape

There was a police-car behind us. In front of us, there was another bend in the road.

'Quick,' said Shirley. 'When we get round the corner, stop immediately. Get out of the car and run round to the other side. We must change places. Then the police will think I was driving. Do you understand?'

'I think so,' I replied.

We went round the corner and stopped. I got out quickly and ran around to the other side of the car. Shirley moved into the driver's seat and I sat in her seat. Then I closed the door.

The police-car came round the corner. It stopped in front of us.

Two policemen got out and came towards the car. One of the policemen put his head through the window. He looked at Shirley's legs first. Then he looked at Shirley and smiled.

'You were going fast, weren't you?' the policeman said to her.

'Was I?' said Shirley. 'I didn't think I was.'

'Perhaps not,' he said, 'but you nearly lost control on that corner. That's why we came after you.'

'Oh,' said Shirley. She pretended to be surprised. 'I'm sorry. I'll be more careful next time.'

'Have you got your licence?' the policeman asked.

'Oh, yes,' Shirley answered. She took it from her bag and gave it to him.

The policeman looked at the licence.

'You were going fast, weren't you?' the policeman said to her.

'Is this your address, in London?' he asked.

I was surprised. Shirley didn't live in London.

'Yes,' she said.

'What are you doing so far from London?' he asked.

'Oh, we're visiting some friends,' she said. She smiled at him again.

'When are you going back to London?' he asked.

'Tomorrow,' she replied. 'I have to go back to work then.'

'Is this your car?' the policeman asked.

'Yes,' she said.

The policeman was interested in Shirley. He didn't know that I had been the driver. Everything was all right.

Then the policeman looked at me.

'Is this your boyfriend?' he asked Shirley.

'Yes,' she said.

'What's your name?' he asked me.

'Tom Russell.' I said. I didn't want to tell him my real name.

'Do you drive too?' he asked me.

Shirley answered. 'No, he doesn't,' she said. 'Why do you think that I'm driving?'

'Well, drive more carefully next time,' the policeman said. 'You don't want to have an accident, do you?'

'No, you're right,' Shirley said. 'Thank you very much.'

The two policemen went back to their car and drove away. Shirley and I sat and looked at each other.

'I can't believe it,' I said. 'We're all right. They didn't see that I was driving.'

'No,' said Shirley. 'We've both got the same colour hair and we're the same height. The police were a long way

36

behind us. They didn't know which was you and which was me.'

I laughed and she gave me a kiss.

'Why did you say your name was Tom Russell?' she asked.

'Well, I didn't want the policeman to tell my parents.'

Shirley shook her head.

'No, Tom,' she said. 'That's not the real reason. You were frightened of the police. Have you been in trouble with the police? Come on, tell me. I won't tell anybody.'

I wanted to tell her and at the same time I didn't want to tell her. I said nothing.

'Tom, you can trust me,' she said. 'Remember, I told the police that you couldn't drive. I told a lie for you.'

That was true. She was a real friend and she wanted to help me.

'I took some money from my father,' I said. 'He never gave me any money. I needed money and I took it. He told the police and I was taken to court. Now I have to go to the police once every month. The police want to know where I am and what I'm doing.'

'I see,' said Shirley. 'When do you have to go to the police again?'

'Ten days from now,' I said.

'Oh, that's all right then,' she said. 'You can do the job for Masters first and then you can go to the police.'

'Yes,' I said. 'I wish Masters was my father. He's much nicer than my real father. What's your father like, Shirley?'

She didn't answer the question.

'Come on,' she said, 'let's go and eat. I'm hungry.'

10

Learning to Use the Scuba Suit

Before breakfast the next morning, I went down to the swimming pool with Masters. He gave me the scuba suit and I put it on. Masters fixed a cylinder of air on my back.

'That's good,' he said. 'And now, the flippers. Put them on your feet.'

Next Masters gave me a big heavy belt.

'This is a special belt,' he said. 'It's very heavy, so that you can go down quickly in the water. When you want to come up again, you take it off.'

Then Masters picked up the face mask.

'Now put this on,' he said. 'You'll find it strange at first.'

I felt a little scared. I felt that I was going into another world.

'You're not frightened, are you?' Masters asked. 'There's no need to worry. You'll soon get used to the mask.'

There was a tube fixed to the air cylinder. He put the end of the tube in my mouth.

Masters explained everything to me slowly and clearly. He showed me how the air supply worked. I turned the air on and off. He showed me everything that I had to do.

'It's really very simple,' he said. 'It seems difficult at first. But it will be very easy when you get used to it.'

'What happens when there is no more air in the cylinder?' I asked.

'Then you must come up quickly!' said Masters. 'But you have enough air for twenty minutes.'

Next, I practised breathing exercises for an hour. I still hadn't gone into the water. I had to practise everything first.

'This is a special belt,' he said. 'It's very heavy, so that you can go down quickly in the water.'

We went and had breakfast. Shirley had breakfast with us. I wanted to talk to her, but Masters was with us all the time.

All morning, Masters and I looked at maps. We studied plans of *The Kular*. I had to know where everything was on the ship.

'It's very dark down in the water,' Masters explained. 'You won't be able to see clearly.'

In the afternoon, we went back to the swimming pool. I put on the scuba suit again. It was easier now. Then I got into the water. Masters came into the water with me.

Suddenly my mask filled with water. I didn't know what to do. I tried to remember what Masters had told me. But it was no good. I waved my arms and tried to shout. I felt very scared. I was sure that I was going to drown. I was going down into the water . . .

Then Masters caught me. He took off my heavy belt and we came up again to the surface. I breathed air again.

Masters looked at me angrily.

'I told you what you must do,' he said. 'Why didn't you remember?'

'I forgot,' I said.

'Well, you mustn't forget,' Masters said. 'You mustn't forget anything. I'm paying you money for this job. It's a lot of money. And it's not a difficult job. But you mustn't make mistakes. You're not stupid. So remember what I say!'

Masters had never been so angry with me before. He was so angry that I felt frightened.

'All right,' Masters said in a quieter voice. 'Now you'd better practise again. Then you'll know what to do.'

Masters explained to me again.

'When your mask is full of water, breathe out through

your nose,' he said. 'That pushes all the water out of the mask. You must hold your mask at the top. Then more water can't get in.'

At the end of the day, I was able to use the scuba suit. But I felt very tired. I was so tired that I went to bed immediately. I didn't see Shirley.

11

A Man Called Lewis

The next day we practised in the swimming pool again. I was getting better and better. We practised all day. At the end, I was not afraid at all. Only one thing still worried me.

'Are you sure I'll have enough air?' I asked.

'There's enough air for you to stay down twenty minutes,' Masters said. 'Twenty minutes is enough time for you to do the job.'

Then he said softly, 'I told Lewis that, too.'

I had never heard of Lewis before.

'Who's Lewis?' I asked.

Masters looked surprised. 'Oh, nobody, nobody at all. I showed him the scuba suit once, that's all.'

Masters stood up and walked away.

I understood that Lewis was important to Masters. But Masters didn't want to tell me about Lewis. Why?

I put my clothes on and went back to the house. I felt happier.

Tomorrow evening I'll have finished the job, I thought. And I'll have my money. I'll be free. Shirley and Masters will see that I can do the job. I'll make a success of it . . . but I won't see Shirley again.

Shirley was sitting watching television. I went to kiss her, but she moved away.

'What's wrong?' I asked her.

'Nothing's wrong,' she said. 'But I don't want to kiss you now. I don't feel in the mood. People have different moods, you know. Sometimes you're happy, sometimes you're unhappy. People can't be the same all the time. I'm not angry with you. But I don't want to kiss you now.'

'But tonight is my last night,' I said to her. 'I'm leaving tomorrow. I won't see you again.'

'Perhaps you will, Tom,' Shirley said. 'You never know.'

I felt very upset now.

'You don't like me, do you?' I shouted. 'You were nice to me because you wanted me to work for Masters. That's it.'

'That's not true, Tom,' she said. 'I like you a lot. I'm sorry, but I don't feel in the mood tonight. It's not your fault. There's nothing wrong with you.'

I suddenly remembered the name Lewis. Did Shirley know Lewis?

'Do you like me more than Lewis?' I asked.

Shirley opened her eyes with surprise.

'What do you know about Lewis?' she asked.

'He worked here, didn't he?' I said. 'He used the scuba suit, didn't he?' I was guessing, of course.

'But how did you know about him?' Shirley asked. 'Did Masters talk about him?'

'Yes, he did,' I said. 'Is Lewis your boyfriend? Is that why you don't want to kiss me?'

'No, he wasn't,' she said. She was nearly crying. 'He was never my boyfriend.'

'I don't believe you,' I said. 'I'm going. I don't want to work for Masters. I don't want you. You can find somebody else for the job.'

'No, Tom, no,' Shirley said. She held me by the hand. 'No, you mustn't go. Forget about Lewis. He's dead.'

I was surprised. Was she telling the truth? I thought she was. I remembered what Masters had said about Lewis. I remembered that he didn't want to talk about Lewis. Lewis was dead.

'Oh, that's all right then,' I said. 'Lewis wasn't your boyfriend.'

'Don't you care that Lewis is dead?' asked Shirley.

'No,' I said. 'I didn't know him. But I care about you.'

She stood up.

'I'm glad you care about me,' she said. 'You must finish the job, Tom. You must do it. When you finish the job, we'll both go away. We'll have a holiday together. That's a good idea, isn't it?'

'Yes,' I said. 'That's a great idea.'

'Just the two of us,' she said. 'I want that very much.'

She kissed me.

'Goodnight,' she said. 'Go to bed now. You'll have to get up early tomorrow.'

I went upstairs to bed. I didn't go to sleep immediately. I lay in bed thinking. Suddenly I remembered something. I hadn't asked Shirley how Lewis had died.

12

The Job Begins

I woke up early the next morning. I looked out of the window. It was raining. I remembered what Shirley had said – 'When you finish the job, we'll both go away.' It was a wonderful idea.

At breakfast, Masters and I sat quietly and drank a cup of tea.

'How do you feel?' he asked me.

'I feel great,' I replied. I smiled at him.

'Is Shirley awake?' I asked. I wanted to see her before we left.

'No,' he said. 'She never wakes up early. But don't worry, Tom. She'll come later. When we've finished the job, she'll be waiting for us. And she'll have some hot coffee for us. She likes you, you know.'

We got into the Jaguar and drove away. I felt happy. I was not afraid of the job. I knew I could do it. And I was happy about Shirley.

It was still raining. There were no other cars on the road. It was still very early. Masters told me again what I had to do. I knew it already, but I listened.

'You must remember one thing, Tom,' he said. 'When you have the diamonds, don't come up again too fast. You must come up slowly through the water. I've told you everything before. But I don't want you to forget. All right?'

I didn't like the way he spoke. He spoke like my father.

'OK,' I said. 'You don't have to tell me again. I know what to do.'

'I hope so,' said Masters. 'You mustn't make any mistakes. One mistake and you may die.'

I knew that. I was going to be very careful.

We stopped at Clark's house. Clark got into the car, and we drove to the sea.

The boat was in a boat-house. Masters, Clark and I took all the things out of the car and put them in the boat. Then Masters and I put on our scuba suits. I was soon ready.

We all got into the boat. Masters started the engine and we moved out to sea.

I looked back at the land. I could see houses, but no people. Everyone must still be asleep, I thought. Nobody was watching us.

Masters looked at the map.

'Here we are,' he said. '*The Kular* must be below us.'

He stopped the engine. A moment later the boat stopped moving. My heart was beating. I looked at Masters. He had a serious expression on his face.

'Are you ready, Tom?' Masters said to me. 'Let's not waste time. Let's go quickly. When we go down, we must stay close to each other, remember.'

I put the air tube in my mouth. Masters did the same. We got into the water and began to go down. Clark stood up in the boat and watched us.

I moved very slowly in the water. Masters was in front of me. It wasn't very dark in the water. A fish swam near to me.

Masters waved his arm. I swam towards him. A moment later I saw the ship. Masters swam down towards a door. I followed close behind him. We stopped at the door. Masters held my arm with one hand. With the other hand, he pointed through the door.

Then Masters and I put on our scuba suits. I was soon ready.

I knew what he meant. He was going to wait for me at the door. I was going inside by myself.

13

Inside *The Kular*

I went through the door. Inside it was very dark. I couldn't see anything. I had a torch with me and I switched it on. But it didn't give much light in the dark water.

I was frightened. I stopped and tried to make myself calm again.

I realised that I was wasting time. How long had I been in the water? I didn't know. Perhaps ten minutes. And I only had enough air in the cylinder for twenty minutes.

I realised something else, too. The ship was not on its side. Masters had said that the ship was lying on its side. He said he had been down several times. But it wasn't on its side. That was strange. Perhaps it had moved in the water.

I went on slowly and carefully. I swam through another door. This door was very narrow. It was half shut and it was impossible to open it any more. I had to be very careful. I didn't want to catch my air tube in the door. I went through very carefully. I put my feet through the opening first. Then I pushed the rest of my body through the opening.

I found myself in a small cabin. I remembered the plans of the boat exactly. I was very close to the diamonds. I was near to success! It was very dark and the torch did not help me much.

There was a seat in front of me. I knew that the diamonds were hidden in this seat. Masters had given me a knife. I took out the knife. But then I saw something in the light of my torch. There was a cut in the seat. Someone else had cut it already.

I was amazed. I didn't believe it. Masters had said that no one else had been inside the ship. I put my hand inside the cut. There was nothing there. The diamonds had gone. Someone had already taken them.

I was worried.

Masters won't believe me, I thought. He'll say I looked in the wrong place.

I didn't know what to do. I had to go back to Masters without the diamonds. I didn't have them and there was no more time to search for them. How much air did I have left? Perhaps enough for five minutes.

I went back to the narrow door. There was something floating in the water behind the door. The light from my torch shone on it.

My heart started beating hard. It was a small bag. There was a red line on it. I recognised it. Masters had said the diamonds were in this bag.

I opened the bag. There were no diamonds inside. There was only some white powder. Some of the white powder had come out of the bag. It was floating like a cloud in the water. But diamonds aren't white. And they don't go cloudy in water.

I pulled the bag and some more white powder came out of it. The bag was caught on something. I pulled hard and it came free. I held it tightly in my hand.

Now I had to get out. I moved fast. I breathed hard and I used a lot of air. How much air did I still have?

As I moved, I was thinking.

Who moved the bag? I asked myself. Where are the diamonds? What happened to the man who found the bag?

I was sure that somebody had been here. Somebody had taken the bag out of the seat. Suddenly I knew the answer. Lewis. Masters had spoken about Lewis. Lewis had seen the scuba suit. And Shirley had said that Lewis was dead.

I was sure of one thing. Lewis had died when he tried to get the diamonds. Was I going to die? My mind was full of terrible thoughts.

I moved as fast as possible. I didn't look where I was going. I hit the door and the air tube came out of my mouth. I was drowning. I found the air tube and put it back in my mouth. But there was no air in it. It was full of water.

My head felt terrible. I could not control myself. My arms went above my head, my head went back . . .

Then suddenly I was breathing air again. I had moved my head back. That was the right thing to do. I had practised that with Masters. I was alive!

Now I had to get out of the ship. I went through the door and started to swim up.

I saw bubbles. I didn't know where they were coming from. Then I remembered Masters. He was waiting for me. I looked in my hands. I didn't have the bag. I had lost it when I was fighting for air. But I didn't care. There weren't any diamonds for Masters.

Masters was holding onto a piece of metal on the side of the ship. When he saw me, he began waving. I swam close to him. He pointed to his air tube with both hands. Then I realised that he wasn't moving in the water. He was caught on something.

I went very close to Masters. He tried to take my air tube out of my mouth. I moved away quickly. I could see his eyes. He looked very frightened. He was trying to kill me.

I moved around Masters carefully. He was still waving at me. He was angry because I didn't have the diamonds. But that was stupid. He didn't know that the diamonds were missing.

I moved behind him. Now I could see better. Masters' air tube was caught round the metal. I tried to free it.

Then Masters stopped moving. The air tube came out of his mouth. A lot of bubbles came out of his mouth. He was drowning.

I pulled hard, and managed to free his air tube. I took off his belt, and then mine. I pulled Masters by the arm and we started to go up to the surface. Now I had to be very careful. I must not go too slowly, or Masters was going to die. But I must not go too fast.

I remembered Masters' words earlier that morning. 'When you have the diamonds, Tom, you must come up slowly through the water.' But now I didn't have any diamonds and Masters was in real trouble.

14

Questions Are Answered

We came up slowly towards the surface. I hoped that Masters was still alive. But I didn't know.

I did know one thing: I had done a good job. I had found the bag. I had saved Masters. I had done these things by myself. Nobody had told me what to do. I was bringing Masters to the surface now. And I was doing this by myself. Now I knew that I could do things by myself.

We got to the surface. We were close to the boat. I took my air tube out of my mouth and shouted to Clark. Now Masters seemed very heavy. I couldn't hold him much longer.

Clark leant over. He put his hands down into the water and took hold of Masters. Clark was very strong. He pulled and Masters came out of the water.

Now I felt very weak and cold. Clark didn't help me, because he was busy with Masters. At last I managed to get into the boat.

Clark was breathing into Masters' mouth. I couldn't help him. I sat in the bottom of the boat and began to shake. I was cold and tired, and also frightened.

Clark took a bottle out of his pocket and gave it to me.

'Here, drink this,' he said. 'It'll do you good.'

I drank some. It made me cough. But then I felt much better.

'How is Masters?' I asked Clark.

'He's dead,' Clark said simply.

I had never seen a dead man before. Masters didn't look dead; he looked tired and asleep. His skin was a little blue and there were dark spots on his hands.

I looked at my hands. There was a cut on the back of one of them. I didn't remember when I had cut myself. My hand was beginning to hurt.

Clark started the engine and the boat began to move.

'Did you find the bag?' Clark asked me.

'Yes,' I said. 'But there were no diamonds in it – only some white powder.'

Clark didn't say anything.

After a moment, I asked, 'What was in the bag, Mr Clark?'

'Drugs, of course,' he replied. 'It was heroin in the bag.'

'But Masters said it was diamonds,' I said.

'I'm not surprised,' said Clark. 'He said diamonds because diamonds are more exciting. And he didn't want you to know, you see.'

I understood what Clark meant.

'Did the heroin belong to Masters?' I asked.

'Yes,' Clark said. 'He didn't want to lose it. But I knew that the search was dangerous. After Lewis died, I told Masters not to try again.'

'We'll have to tell the police, won't we?' I said. 'Will there be trouble?'

'No,' Clark said. 'Masters drowned. Only you and I and Shirley know about the drugs. He didn't tell anyone else. We'll say that it was an accident. You can say he was looking at the wreck. Lots of people go down and look at wrecks.'

We were close to the land now. I looked and I saw the Mini at the edge of the water. Shirley was waiting for us.

'It'll be a terrible shock for Shirley,' I said. 'She'll have to find a new job now.'

'Yes,' said Clark, 'but she won't find a new father, will she?'

'A father?' I asked. I didn't understand.

'Didn't you know?' said Clark. 'Masters was her father. Didn't they tell you?'

I had never thought that Masters was Shirley's father. She had always called him Masters.

Now I realised how Masters had known so much about me. Shirley had told him everything. Masters had told her to be friendly to me. They had wanted me to do the job.

I felt upset. Shirley was my only friend. But was she a real friend?

'Was Shirley friendly with Lewis?' I asked Clark.

'No, not really,' Clark said.

'What happened when Lewis died?' I asked. 'What did the police do?'

'No one ever found him. The police don't know that he died,' Clark said. 'We took him out to sea. We put a heavy belt around him and threw his body in the water.'

Now I could see Shirley very clearly. She was standing at the edge of the water. She seemed quiet and calm. I didn't wave to her.

She knows that something is wrong because she can't see her father, I thought.

The boat reached land. Shirley stood for a long time and looked down at her father. She didn't say anything.

'I'm sorry, very sorry,' Clark said to her.

I saw the tears in Shirley's eyes.

She turned to me.

'How did it happen?' she asked after some time.

I told her the whole story. She listened and didn't ask any questions.

56

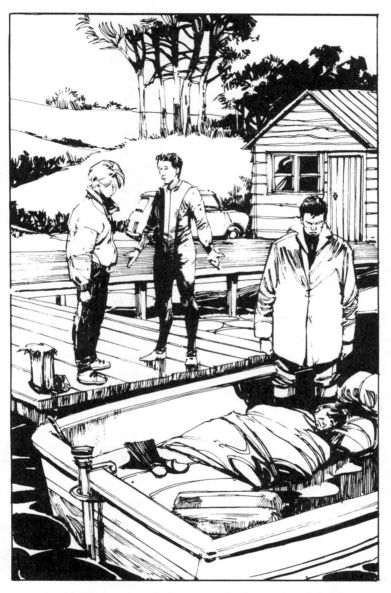

I told Shirley the whole story. She listened and didn't ask any questions.

'But I couldn't help him,' I said. 'I couldn't do anything.'
She tried to smile.

'I know, Tom,' she said. 'I'm sure you did your best. But you don't have much experience. He didn't have much, either. He was a brave man. He went down with you, but he didn't like swimming.'

'You're right,' I said. 'Your father was a brave man.'

'So you know about us,' said Shirley. 'Masters *was* my father. I didn't like telling you lies about him. But he said that you mustn't know. But Tom, I do like you. I like you a lot.'

I knew that she meant it.

'Shirley,' I said. 'Can we still go away together?'

'Oh, yes,' she replied. 'I need to be with you now, Tom. I haven't a mother or a father now. I only have you.'

'Haven't you got any other friends or relatives?' I asked.

The tears began to run down her face. I wanted to look after her.

'No,' she said. 'I have no one, no one except you, Tom. I need somebody brave. You were brave today. I don't want to be alone. And you don't want to be alone, do you?'

'No,' I said. I had been alone too long. I put my arms around her.

'But we must go to the police first,' she said. 'We must tell them that there has been an accident. We won't tell them about the drugs. I want to forget about the drugs, don't you? I want us to have a new start. Is that how you feel, Tom?'

'Yes, yes it is,' I said. And I meant it.

Points for Understanding

1

1 Who were the two people in the car?
2 Why didn't Tom want to work in an office?
3 Were Tom's parents alive?

2

1 What do we know about Tom's size and strength?
2 What did Masters offer Tom?

3

1 What did Masters tell Tom about the job?
2 Why was Tom pleased that Shirley's room was so near?

4

1 Shirley asked Tom to do two things in the pool. What things?
2 Why did Tom want Shirley to be friendly?
3 Did Tom know Shirley's real job?
4 Did Tom know how Masters had become rich?

5

1 What was Masters doing while Tom was in the pool?
2 What business did Masters say he was in? When will we learn what this means?
3 What happened to Tom's bag of clothes?

6

1 What did Masters say was in the sunken ship?
2 What was Tom's job?
3 Why did Tom ask for more money?
4 Why did Masters visit Mr Clark?
5 What did Tom promise to do?

7

1 Why was it wrong for Tom to drive a car?
2 Why did Masters want Tom to phone his father?

8

1 What was following the Mini?
2 Why was Tom worried?

9

1 Who was more frightened of the police: Tom or Shirley?
2 What did Tom have to do in ten days' time?
3 Did Shirley ever talk about her father?

10

1 How long did the air in the cylinder last?
2 Why did Tom have to study plans of the sunken ship?

11

1 Why did Shirley tell Tom to forget about Lewis?
2 What were Shirley and Tom going to do after the job?

12

1 What did Masters warn Tom to do when he got the diamonds?
2 Why didn't Tom like the way Masters spoke?
3 What did Masters mean when he pointed through the door?

13

1 When Tom saw the cut in the seat, he was surprised. Why?
2 What was inside the small bag?
3 How did Tom think that Lewis had died?
4 What had happened to Masters?

14

1 What was really in the bag?
2 Why had Masters said it was diamonds?
3 What did Tom learn about Masters and Shirley?
4 Was Shirley a real friend to Tom?

Road to Nowhere *by John Milne*
The Black Cat *by John Milne*
Don't Tell Me What To Do *by Michael Hardcastle*
The Runaways *by Victor Canning*
The Red Pony *by John Steinbeck*
The Goalkeeper's Revenge and Other Stories *by Bill Naughton*
The Stranger *by Norman Whitney*
The Promise *by R.L. Scott-Buccleuch*
The Man With No Name *by Evelyn Davies and Peter Town*
The Cleverest Person in the World *by Norman Whitney*
Claws *by John Landon*
Z for Zachariah *by Robert C. O'Brien*
Tales of Horror *by Bram Stoker*
Frankenstein *by Mary Shelley*
Silver Blaze and Other Stories *by Sir Arthur Conan Doyle*
Tales of Ten Worlds *by Arthur C. Clarke*
The Boy Who Was Afraid *by Armstrong Sperry*
Room 13 and Other Ghost Stories *by M.R. James*
The Narrow Path *by Francis Selormey*
The Woman in Black *by Susan Hill*

For further information on the full selection of
Readers at all five levels in the series, please refer
to the Heinemann Guided Readers catalogue.

Heinemann English Language Teaching
A division of Heinemann Publishers (Oxford) Ltd
Halley Court, Jordan Hill, Oxford OX2 8EJ

OXFORD   MADRID   ATHENS   PARIS   FLORENCE   PRAGUE
SÃO PAULO   CHICAGO   MELBOURNE   AUCKLAND
SINGAPORE   TOKYO   GABORONE
JOHANNESBURG   PORTSMOUTH (NH)   IBADAN

ISBN 0 435 27189 X

Don't Tell Me What To Do was first published in Great Britain in 1970 by
William Heinemann Ltd in the Pyramid Series
This retold version for Heinemann Guided Readers
© Philip King 1975, 1992
First published 1975
Reprinted nine times
This edition published 1992

Illustrated by Bob Harvey
Typography by Adrian Hodgkins
Cover by Ben Fowler and Threefold Design
Typeset in 11.5/14.5 pt Goudy
by Joshua Associates Ltd, Oxford
Printed and bound in Malta by Interprint Limited

94   95   96   97   10   9   8   7   6   5   4